The Greatness of Christ

W M Henry

ISBN: 978-1-78364-462-9

The Open Bible Trust
Fordland Mount, Upper Basildon,
Reading, RG8 8LU, UK.

www.obt.org.uk

The Greatness of Christ

Contents

Page

1.
INTRODUCTION

INTRODUCTION

The Lord Jesus Christ is regarded in many different ways by men.

Some consider Him to have been a great teacher: one who showed us that we should love one another, help those who are in need by sharing our possessions with them and not retaliate when we are wronged. Unfortunately He was misunderstood, betrayed and finally executed.

To others He was the perfect man who showed us by His life the way that we should live – a man who was at one with Himself; who was resolute in purpose and would not be diverted from the goals He had set for Himself. He retained this unity of purpose right to the end refusing to compromise Himself even in the face of death.

To political extremists He was a revolutionary who championed the cause of the people and was murdered by the political and religious establishment of His day. So He is placed on a par with Russell, Buddha or Guevara depending on one's outlook.

To Christians, He is the Son of God who gave Himself for the sin of the world; but how much do we really appreciate of the full glories of Christ?

As children in Sunday School we learn and sing of "Gentile Jesus Meek and Mild" and as we grow up there is a tendency for this image to remain. He is viewed as the one who welcomed little children, and wept with compassion at the grave of Lazarus and over Jerusalem. To some there is a hint of weakness or sentimentality there, and it can tend to color our view of Him.

Many believers who appreciate the work done by the Lord on the cross still spend much of their time considering the earthly stage of His existence, and there is a danger that, by concentrating their efforts on the Lord's ministry at that time, they fail to appreciate the nature of their Lord and Saviour to the full. Paradoxically, the writings which raise the Lord Jesus Christ to the highest place are not those which contain His words and deeds. The full glories of Christ are revealed by the letters of the apostle Paul, though there are references in the Gospel writings to many of the points developed by the apostle of the Gentiles.

In this publication we will consider some aspects of the greatness of the Lord Jesus Christ as revealed in the New Testament.

We will begin by examining the greatness of the Lord in eternity past – before He came to the earth and "lived for a while among us". Then we will study the divine attributes which he displayed during His earthly life, and, finally, we will consider His resurrection greatness – present and future- in relation to God's earthly and heavenly purposes.

It is not possible to exhaust such a subject in so brief a study, but by considering the main themes we can perhaps appreciate more fully the One who "is all, and is in all". (Colossians 3:11).

2.
HIS
GREATNESS
IN THE PAST

HIS GREATNESS IN THE PAST

The opening verses of John's Gospel take us back to "the beginning", and in the first verse of that Gospel we read of the Lord Jesus Christ:

> "In the beginning was the Word, and the Word was with God, and the Word was God. He was with God in the beginning."

That John was referring to Christ is confirmed in verse 14, where he states "the Word became flesh and lived for a while among us."

The Lord Jesus was in existence with God before all else – at the very beginning. And not only was He *with* God, but He *was* God. Before the creation of the world He was in a position of identity with God, with all the glory which that entailed. In John Chapter 17 we read the Lord's Prayer to His Father, prior to His arrest, and there He requests that the Father will;

"... glorify me in your presence with the glory I had with you before the world began." (verse 5)

Again, in verse 24 of the same chapter He prays for His disciples and all future believers that they may be with Him where He is:

"... to see my glory, the glory you have given me because you loved me before the creation of the world."

The Lord Jesus, then, was looking forward to His restoration to the glory He had in times past.

But not only does John establish the Lord's deity and eternal existence in his opening verse; he gives Him a title – "the Word." This is a translation of the Greek word *logos* which has two meanings: it can mean "word" or "reason" – which are connected, since the spoken word is the expression of the thought processes of the mind. To the Jews the Word of God was something powerful. Jeremiah says:

"'Is not my word like fire,' declares the Lord, 'and like a hammer that breaks a rock in pieces?' " (Jeremiah 23:29)

And the Lord Jesus was the Word of God. William Barclay says

> "'The Word became flesh' might well be translated 'the mind of God became a human person.'" (*The Gospels and Acts* Volume II, page 147).

To the Greek the word *logos* denoted a kind of divine law which holds the universe together preventing chaos from taking over in a world in a state of constant flux. The use of this term to describe the Lord Jesus Christ would therefore be meaningful to both John's Jewish and Greek readers. But he is not using this idea merely to present his theology in terms of contemporary philosophy. Its abstract concept found reality in the person of the lord Jesus Christ.

John goes on to say: "Through him all things were made" (John 1:3). If we turn back to the Genesis account of the creation we read that each stage of the creation took place at the spoken Word of God (e.g. Genesis 1:3, 6, 9). The world as we know it was created through God's Word – the *logos* – and that Word was the Lord Jesus Christ. The writer to the Hebrews, in his opening verses, takes up the theme of the Lord Jesus being the creating power of God:

> "In these last days he has spoken to us by his Son, whom he appointed heir of all things, and through whom he made the universe." (Hebrews 1:2)

In his letter to the Colossians, Paul goes further by declaring that the Lord is: "the firstborn over all creation" (Colossians 1:15). This title "firstborn" is a term which could be confusing. "First" is to be understood in terms of priority in rank rather than in time. The use of the term "born" is also misleading as it suggests a time when He did not exist, yet John in the opening verses of his Gospel points out that this was not the case. He was in the beginning with God. Paul is not saying that the Lord Jesus was the first to be born or to be created.

He is firstborn over all creation because "by him all things were created" (Colossians 1:16). So this title is given to the Lord in consequence of His work as creator. He is supreme over all because He created all. The New English Bible renders this: "his is the primacy over all created things."

In his book *The Church Epistles* E.W. Bullinger translates "first born" as "heir" (as Hebrews 1:2 says), and this leads on to what Paul says at the end of verse 16 of the first chapter of Colossians. Not only were all things created *by* Him, but all things were created *for* Him. He is not only the agent of creation, He is the goal of all creation. Colossians 1:16 gives us an indication of what is involved here:

> "… by him all things were created; things in heaven and on earth, visible and invisible, whether thrones or powers or rulers or authorities; all things were created by him and for him."

Here we have a list covering not only the visible world around us, but the invisible world also. All of these beings, hostile as some are to the Lord and His work, were created by Him and for Him. John sums up the position in his gospel by saying:

> "… without him nothing was made that has been made." (1:3)

This was the position of the Lord Jesus Christ in ages past. In the beginning He was with God and He was God. He was the means by which God created all that has been created, the eternal logos – God's word in action – and He was the one for whom all things were created. He was the heir, the head over the entire creation, and equal to God with all the glory that accompanied such a position.

But He did not consider that the glory that related to the position of equality with God was something to be held on to at all costs. In Philippians chapter 2, Paul uses the Lord Jesus Christ as an example to believers of how they should live. Paul says of the Lord:

"… who being in very nature God, did not consider equality with God something to be grasped, but made himself nothing, taking the very nature of a servant." (Philippians 2:6, 7).

He was in very nature God, and He exchanged that nature for the nature of a servant. This 'Nature" does not refer to His outward appearance, as this has little meaning when applied to God, nor to His essence since He did not shed Himself of His deity when He "became flesh and lived for a while among us". It refers to His status – the position that went with equality with God. This is what He abandoned, replacing it with the status of a servant.

For Him, equality with God was not "some-thing to be grasped" (the word comes from a root meaning "plunder" or "rob" – hence the Authorized Version "thought it not robbery to be equal with God"). The question arises as to whether Paul meant that equality with God was something the Lord already possessed, or something that He hoped to possess in the future.

Commenting on the Revised Version rendering: "Counted it not a prize to be on an equality with God," W. E. Vine says

> "The form 'to be' is ambiguous and easily lends itself to the erroneous notion that to be on equality with God was something to be acquired in the future. The rendering 'counted it not a prize that He was on an equality with God', is quite as accurate and more free from ambiguity." (*Expository Dictionary of New Testament Words* – Vol. III page 215).

The Lord did not consider that this position was a prize that He should hold on to at all costs. He was prepared to abandon His status to secure our salvation.

The contrast between the second Adam and the first Adam is too apparent to be unintentional. In the Garden of Eden, Adam and Eve ate the forbidden fruit, not only because it was attractive to look at, but also because it was "desirable for gaining wisdom" (Genesis 3:6). This was in response to the serpent's lie:

> "… when you eat of it … you will be like God, knowing good and evil." (verse 5)

Adam, then, seeking the position that was not his, believed the lie and fell, while the Lord Jesus Christ, in the position of equality with God by right, did not consider this a prize to be held on to, but laid aside the glories that went with His position and took upon Himself "human likeness". Thus the greatness of the Lord Jesus is demonstrated, not only in the position that was His by right, but in the fact that He was prepared to lay aside the glories of that position to accomplish the purpose of God. Paul goes on in the second chapter of Philippians, to show the extent of the Lord's self-emptying:

> "And being found in appearance as a man, he humbled himself and became obedient to death – even death on a cross." (Philippians 2:8)

The Lord's life on the earth was characterized by His obedience. He took on Himself the status of a servant, and as such He declared to the Jews:

> "… the Son can do nothing by himself; he can do only what he sees his Father doing, because whatever the Father does the Son also does." (John 5:19)

And later He declares:

> "I seek not to please myself but him who sent me." (John 5:30)

This obedience reached its pinnacle with His willingness to go all the way to the cross if that be His Father's will. Prior to His arrest we see Him in the Garden of Gethsemane, well aware of what lay before Him, and His prayer for deliverance was qualified by His dedication to obedience to the Father:

> "Father, if you are willing, take this cup from me; yet not my will, but yours be done." (Luke 22:42)

Later, strengthened by an angel, He rebuked Peter for attacking the High Priest's servant with the words:

> "Shall I not drink the cup the Father has given me?" (John 18:11)

In Matthew's version of the same incident the Lord declares:

> "Do you think I cannot call on my Father, and he will at once put at my disposal more than twelve legions of angels: But how then would the Scriptures be fulfilled that say it must happen in this way?" (Matthew 26:53-54)

His obedience to the Father's will was complete. "He became obedient unto death – even death on a cross"

* * * *

Why was all that necessary? It was the Father's purpose that the Lord should shed His blood, and

Paul explains why in the first chapter of Colossians. In verse 19 he says:

> "For God was pleased to have all his fullness dwell in him, and through him to reconcile to himself all things, whether things on earth or things in heaven, by making peace through His blood, shed on the cross."

The making of peace and the reconciling of all things were accomplished through the shedding of His blood. This is an echo of what the apostle had written earlier to the Romans:

> "Since we have now been justified by his blood, how much more shall we be saved from God's wrath through him! For if, when we were God's enemies we were reconciled to him through the death of his Son, how much more, having been reconciled, shall we be saved through his life!" (Romans 5:9, 10)

- having been justified by His blood – we shall be saved.
- having been reconciled by His death – we shall be saved.

Again peace has been made and reconciliation accomplished by the Lord's blood shed on the cross. Further, in Colossians 1:21-22 we read:

> "Once you were alienated from God and were enemies in your minds because of your evil behavior. But now he has reconciled you by Christ's physical body through death to present you holy in his sight."

And not only are individuals reconciled to God by Christ's actions, but Jew and Gentile are reconciled together through Him. The barrier between them has been broken down and they are united in one body. Ephesians Chapter 2 verse 14 says:

> "For he himself is our peace, who has made the two one and has destroyed the barrier,

the dividing wall of hostility, by abolishing in his flesh the law with its commandments and regulations. His purpose was to create in himself one new man out of the two, thus making peace, and in this one body to reconcile both of them to God through the cross, by which he put to death their hostility."

The climax of God's revelation is the truth concerning the Church which is the Body of Christ, and in Ephesians 3 Paul declares that God's intention is to reveal His manifold wisdom through the Church:

> "… according to his eternal purpose which he accomplished in Christ Jesus our Lord." (Ephesians 3:11)

If He had not been able to do this, there would have been no peace, no reconciliation, and only condemnation for sinful man. The prerequisite was the obedience of the lord Jesus Christ. He came to do the will of His Father and this He did right to the very end.

As we examine the teaching of the Scriptures on the greatness of the Lord Jesus Christ before His incarnation, we see Him existing from the beginning, in a position of equality with God, the Creator of all things, Lord and heir over His creation. Yet His greatness is also demonstrated in the way He was prepared to set all His glory aside to accomplish God's purpose for His fallen world.

3.
HIS
GREATNESS
ON THE EARTH

HIS GREATNESS ON THE EARTH

We have considered the greatness of the Lord Jesus Christ in eternity past, and how He was prepared to lay His glory aside when He came to earth. Philippians 2 states that He:

> "… made himself nothing, taking the very nature of a servant, being made in human likeness." (verse 7)

But this did not mean that He abandoned all His attributes of deity. There are certain aspects of His nature which are unchanging and which shone through very clearly during His life on earth.

The first chapter of Colossians states that:

> "He is the image of the invisible God." (verse 15)

This seems almost a contradiction in terms, but J.B. Lightfoot in his commentary on Colossians states that the Greek word *eikon* translated "image" has the obvious notion of likeness, but also involves two other ideas:

1. Representation – *"eikon* implies an archtype of which it is a copy ... The *eikon* might be the result of a direct imitation like the head of a sovereign on a coin, or it might be due to natural causes like the parental features in the child but in any case it was *derived* from its prototype." (*The Epistles of St. Paul: Colossians and Philemon* Page 145)

There is nothing in the word which implies a *perfect* image. For example, man was made in the image of God, but in the case of the Lord Jesus Christ the fact that the representation *was* perfect can be inferred from the content of Colossians 1. The Lord was a perfect representation of God the Father. But the word *eikon* has another meaning also:

2. Manifestation. Since God is invisible, in order for us to see what He is like, we require a revelation or a manifestation of Him in tangible form. We have this in the Lord Jesus Christ. Colossians 2 tells us:

> For in Christ all the fullness of the Deity lives *in bodily form.*" (verse 9)

He is a visible expression of the invisible God. The same idea is brought out in the first chapter of Hebrews:

> "The Son is the radiance of God's glory and the exact representation of his being, sustaining all things by his powerful word." (Hebrews 1:3)

John, in introducing us to the incarnate Word at the start of his gospel, points out:

> "No-one has ever seen God, but God the only Son, who is at the Father's side, has made him known." (John 1:18)

In the same gospel, the Lord declared his identification with His Father to the Pharisees, who asked Him: "where is your Father?"

> "You do not know me or my Father," Jesus replied. "If you knew me, you would know my Father also." (John 8:19)

Later, as the disciples were comforted by the Lord, Philip requested:

> "Lord, show us the Father and that will be enough for us."

The Lord's reply set forth the position:

> "Don't you know me, Philip, even after I have been among you such a long time? Anyone who has seen me has seen the Father. How can you say, 'Show us the Father'? Don't you believe that I am in the Father, and that the Father is in me?" (John 14:8-10)

The Lord Jesus Christ certainly came to earth to do the will of His Father and was subject to Him at all times; but in another sense He came as the "exact representation" of His Father, to show us what God was like, not only in terms of His love and justice, but in terms of His very being.

* * * *

In Colossians 1:17, Paul makes the statement that Christ "is before all things". He is speaking here of the creating and sustaining power of Christ, so is referring to His priority in time rather than in rank. This makes Paul's use of the present tense of the verb all the more striking. He is showing not only that the Lord existed in the past before all things, but also that His existence is timeless – the very existence of God. In the last chapter of Revelation the Lord Jesus describes Himself as:

> "… the Alpha and the Omega, the First and the Last, the Beginning and the End." (Revelation 22:13)

In the first chapter of that book, we read:

"I am the Alpha and the Omega," says the Lord God; "who is, and who was, and who is to come, the Almighty." (Revelation 1:8)

The Lord Jesus Christ stands outside of time. He knows the end from the beginning. He is from eternity, to eternity. And when He walked this earth, this aspect of His nature was always with Him. In John chapter 8, as the Jews disputed with Him about His claims, the Lord stated:

"Your father Abraham rejoiced at the thought of seeing my day; he saw it and was glad."

The Jews response was predictable:

"You are not yet fifty years old…and you have seen Abraham!" "I tell you the truth," Jesus answered, "before Abraham was born, I am!" (John 8:57-58)

Both in John and in Colossians the Lord's timelessness is demonstrated by His use of the present tense. But there is more. The Jew's reaction was to pick up stones to stone Him, not because He claimed to have predated Abraham but because He was claiming to be God. He took upon Himself the name "I AM", the name by which God introduced Himself to Moses in Exodus 3:14, a name which suggested God's continual unchanging presence through changing generations. The Lord explained Himself to Moses in the next verse:

> "Say to the Israelites, 'The Lord, the God of your fathers – the God of Abraham, the God of Isaac, and the God of Jacob – has sent me to you.' This is my name for ever, the name by which I am to be remembered from generation to generation." (Exodus 3:15)

God's explanation emphasized his unchangeableness through time, and the Lord Jesus Christ by applying this name to Himself, shows His identification with His Father in this respect.

The power of the Lord Jesus Christ, while on earth, to see the end from the beginning is particularly demonstrated in His ability to prophesy. In Matthew 12, He predicted His death and resurrection in picture form by using the simile of Jonah in the belly of the fish:

"... as Jonah was three days and three nights in the belly of a huge fish, so the Son of Man will be three days and three nights in the heart of the earth." (verse 40)

In chapter 16 he repeated His prediction to His disciples more plainly this time, to Peter's consternation (16:21-22).

In Matthew 24 and 25 the Lord foretells the events which will surround the destruction of Jerusalem, and beyond that, the end of the age. His prophecy concerning Jerusalem was fulfilled in A.D. 70, so precisely that several modern commentators have declared that Matthew's Gospel could not have been written until after that date.

Further, the Lord was able to predict His betrayal (Matthew 26:21) and Peter's denial (Matthew 26:34).

These are only examples, for the Lord's earthly life is characterized by His awareness of what lies in the future, yet, as we have seen, he did not shrink from what was before Him, but was prepared to be obedient to the point of death on a cross.

* * * *

There is another aspect of the Lord's earthly life which demonstrates His greatness – the extent of His knowledge. In Colossians 2, Paul states: 'in whom (Christ) are hidden all the treasures of wisdom and knowledge." This is spoken of the glorified Lord Jesus, but, as we examine the record of His life given to us in the Gospels, we cannot fail to notice that the knowledge and wisdom He displayed went far beyond any that could have been learned in His youth as a carpenter's son in Nazareth.

We find the boy Jesus, at the age of twelve, in the Temple Courts with the teachers of the law, listening to them and asking them questions, and already He was displaying extraordinary knowledge.

> "Everyone who heard him was amazed at his understanding and his answers." (Luke 2:47)

After He had commenced His ministry, the Lord visited His home town of Nazareth and there He taught in the synagogue. The result was that all who heard Him were amazed:

> "'Where did this man get these things?' they asked. 'What's this wisdom that has been given him, that he even does miracles! Isn't this the carpenter? Isn't this Mary's son and the brother of James, Joses, Judas and Simon...' And they took offence at him." (Mark 6:2-3).

Those who knew Him well realized that it had been impossible for Him to learn what He knew through normal channels.

Later, as He reasoned with the Pharisees, He saw through their trap on the question of paying tribute to Caesar, and when they heard His reply: "they were amazed. So they left him and went away." (Matthew 22:23). In the same chapter, as the Pharisees and Sadducees questioned Him, the Lord turned the tables and asked them a question about Christ. The result was that:

> "… no-one could say a word in reply, and from that day on no-one dared to ask him any more questions." (Matthew 22:46)

Throughout His life the Lord demonstrated His superior wisdom, not just in teaching and in answering the trick questions of the Pharisees, but in His dealings with individuals. He astounded the woman at the well by what He told her. She declared to her neighbors:

> "Come, see a man who told me everything I ever did." (John 4:29)

Yet it was to this woman that the Lord chose to reveal that He was Messiah (John 4:26), whereas in the previous chapter, when speaking with Nicodemus, He responded to Nicodemus' suggestion that He was "a teacher who has come from God" by saying:

> "… unless a man is born again, he cannot see the kingdom of God" (John 3:3).

One would have thought that He would have discussed His Messiahship with Nicodemus, especially after such an opportunity was presented, and taught the woman about the spiritual rebirth. But the Lord, knowing His listeners and their needs, did not do so. In the second chapter of John we read that the lord would not entrust Himself to men:

> "… for he knew all men. He did not need man's testimony about man, for he knew what was in a man," (John 2:24-25)

The Lord demonstrated the depth of His knowledge and His wisdom in dealing with those in need and those who opposed Him. This wisdom came not from His schooling, but from that store of knowledge which is His as the eternal Word.

* * * *

In the first chapter of Colossians, Paul, speaking of the lord Jesus, says:

> "In him all things hold together." (Colossians 1:17)

The same idea appears in Hebrews 1, where we read of the Son:

> "… sustaining all things by his powerful word." (Hebrews 1:3)

He is the creator, as we have seen, but He is more than that. It is through His power that the creation is maintained. Natural laws which hold the universe together are an expression of the mind of Christ. The Greek *logos* principle operates to give cohesion to otherwise unrelated elements of the world. He has power over His creation, and when He walked the earth He demonstrated it.

He had power over disease. Time after time we read of Him healing all manner of sickness. Many specific examples are given – leprosy, blindness, deafness, fever or paralysis. In other cases, for example in Mark 1:34 we simply read "Jesus healed many who had various diseases."

He even had power over death, raising Jairus' daughter (Mark 5), and the widow's son (Luke 7), as well as His friend Lazarus (John 11). At the grave of Lazarus he wept, not from sorrow at His friend's death as the Jews thought, but with anger and sadness at the effect of the sin and evil in the world which had caused death. As the creator and sustainer, He was the giver of life, and He opposed the effects of evil wherever He saw it.

The miracles we have just considered showed His power over "natural" illnesses, but, where Satan and his host were directly involved, His opposition to them was no less successful. The gospels give us many instances of demons being cast out. They knew who He was, and His power over them was total. In Matthew 8:16 we read that:

"… many who were demon-possessed were brought to him, and he drove out the spirits with a word."

In the same chapter we have the incident of the Gadarene swine, where the demons besought the Lord to be permitted to enter the herd of pigs. The Lord's power over demons was such that people asked:

"Could this be the Son of David?" (Matthew 12:23)

The Pharisees' desperate response was that He drove out demons by Beelzebub, the Prince of Demons, but, as the Lord pointed out, this was impossible. As the Lord walked His earth He saw it marred by Satan's work, either directly, in the possession of men and women, or indirectly, in sickness and disease brought about by Adam's fall, and He opposed this at every turn, not only as a sign to the Jews, but in response to the needs He met.

The Lord's power over His creation was also demonstrated in His control over the elements and in His ability to suspend natural laws. As He crossed the lake with His disciples, he slept through the storm until the disciples, fearing that they were going to be swamped, woke Him.

> "Then he got up and rebuked the winds and the waves, and it was completely calm. The men were amazed and asked, 'What kind of man is this? Even the winds and the waves obey him!'" (Matthew 8:26-27)

In John 6, after He had just fed five thousand people with five loaves and two fish, He walked on the water to meet His disciples in the boat. Not surprisingly, they were terrified, but He reassured them. But the Lord did more than walk on the water, When the disciples prepared to take Him into the boat:

> "… immediately the boat reached the shore where they were heading" (John 6:21).

This was not natural. In Matthew's account of the incident, Peter was encouraged to walk on the water to meet the Lord, and he seems to have been successful until he reached the point where he saw the wind and was afraid (Matthew 14:30). As he sank, the Lord caught him with His hand and rebuked him for doubting. When they climbed into the boat, again we read "the wind died down" leaving the disciples filled with awe at the One in their company.

As the time approached of the Lord's sacrifice of Himself, we have the highly symbolic incident of the cursing of the fig tree, a picture of Israel, for not bearing fruit (Matthew 21:18-22). The result was startling:

> "Immediately the tree withered. When the disciples saw this, they were amazed. 'How did the fig-tree wither so quickly?' they asked."

The fig tree withered because of the power of the Lord. And that power was being offered to the disciples, not only to walk on water but to the extent of moving mountains, if only they would believe it. That power remains with the Lord. He is the sustainer of the world, and it is His world. This thought should be a comfort to us as we see the potentially destructive forces in the hands of twenty-first century man.

When the Lord came to earth, He laid aside the glories of His position of equality with God, but we can still see His greatness as the exact representation of His Father, in His timelessness, His knowledge, His power and His love.

3.

HIS GREATNESS IN RESURRECTION

HIS GREATNESS IN RESURRECTION

1. IN GOD'S EARTHLY PURPOSE

We have considered the power of the Lord Jesus Christ which He demonstrated when He walked this earth, but not all His glories have been revealed to the earth at this time in the unfolding of God's purpose. God's plans for the earth will not be achieved until it is delivered out of the hand of Satan and restored to its rightful owner. In order to understand how this will be realized it is necessary to examine the nature of God's earthly purpose as revealed in Scripture.

God's purpose for the earth, as revealed to Abraham, was that he and his descendants would be blessed by God and would be a means of blessing to "all peoples on earth" (Genesis 26:3,4) and to Jacob (Genesis 28:13-14). The Old Testament shows us God's preparation of the people of Israel for this purpose. They were a favored nation and they were to administer God's blessing to the other inhabitants of the earth. At the head of the nation would be their King – of the line of David. When David was contemplating building a temple for the Lord, he was forbidden to do so, but God made him this promise through the mouth of the prophet Nathan.

> "When your days are over and you rest with your fathers, I will raise up your offspring to succeed you, who will come from your own body, and I will establish his kingdom." (2 Samuel 7:12)

It is apparent that the Lord was looking beyond the establishment of Solomon on the throne, because Nathan continues in verse 16:

> "... your house and your kingdom shall endure for ever before me; your throne shall be established forever."

Although this endless rule did not begin with Solomon, the prophets anticipated the day when the Kingdom of the Son of David would be set up. Isaiah 11 sets the scene:

> "A shoot will come up from the stump of Jesse; from his roots a Branch will bear fruit. The Spirit of the Lord will rest on him – the Spirit of wisdom and of understanding, the Spirit of counsel and of power, the Spirit of knowledge and of the fear of the Lord – and he will delight in the fear of the Lord." (verses 1-3)

This branch to come from the stump of Jesse will administer justice, not only to the people of Israel but all over the world:

> "... with righteousness he will judge the needy, with justice he will give decisions for the poor of the earth. He will strike the earth with the rod of his mouth; with the breath of his lips he will slay the wicked." (verse 4)

The universal nature of His reign is taken up again in verse 10:

"In that day the Root of Jesse will stand as a banner for the peoples; the nations will rally to him, and his place of rest will be glorious."

Conditions for living will be ideal in that day. In verses 6-8 the prophet paints a picture of animals and humans living in perfect harmony with one another. The description culminates in verse 9 with the declaration:

"They will neither harm nor destroy on all my holy mountain,"

Which shows that the nation of Israel in general, and Mount Zion in particular, will be the most privileged place on the earth, but Isaiah goes on to show the world-wide influence of the Kingdom:

"for the earth will be full of the knowledge of the Lord as the waters cover the sea."

What a picture that presents! We see a just government being administered world-wide, and there will be a restoration (at least in some measure) of the conditions lost at the fall, as creatures live in harmony and the length of human life is extended (as Isaiah tells us in chapter 65 verse 20). But it is important to observe that all is not peace and tranquility. There is judgment on the earth. It is clear that those who are evil and oppose the King will be destroyed. David was a prophet as well as a king, and many of his Psalms speak of the days of this Kingdom in terms of judgment. Psalm 110 opens with:

> "The Lord says to my Lord: 'Sit at my right hand until I make your enemies a footstool for your feet'. The Lord will extend your mighty scepter from Zion; rule in the midst of your enemies." (verses 1-2)

The one of whom David spoke was to be greater than David. Not only was He to be a prophet and a King like his father, He was to be a priest as well. The only other person ever to combine these offices was Melchizedek, so David says in verse 4 of the same Psalm:

"The Lord has sworn and will not change his mind: 'You are a priest for ever, in the order of Melchizedek.'"

The remainder of the Psalm shows the king/priest dispensing judgment and punishment to His enemies. Psalm 2 also reveals a world hostile to God and His ways. But God laughs and then declares:

"I have installed my King on Zion, my holy `hill." (verse 6)

God continues:

"You are my Son; today I have become your Father. Ask of me, and I will make the nations your inheritance, the ends of the earth your possession. You will rule them with an iron scepter; you will dash them to pieces like pottery." (verses 7-9)

None of these prophecies has been fulfilled. On a natural level their realization seems more remote than ever before, but the New Testament is clear that they *will* be fulfilled, and the coming Son of David is the Lord Jesus Christ. Matthew opens his Gospel by linking the Lord Jesus with both Abraham (to whom the promises were originally made) and David (the head of the royal line).

> "A record of the genealogy of Jesus Christ the son of David, the son of Abraham." (Matthew 1:1)

In chapter 2 of the same Gospel the wise men asked Herod:

> "Where is the one who has been born King of the Jews?" (verse 2)

At the end of His earthly life, the inscription over the cross read:

> "This is Jesus, the King of the Jews." (Matthew 27:37)

Peter, on the Day of Pentecost, demonstrated clearly that David's prophecies related to the Lord Jesus Christ:

"But he (David) was a prophet and knew that God had promised him on oath that he would place one of his descendants on his throne. Seeing what was ahead, he spoke of the resurrection of the Christ, that he was not abandoned to the grave, nor did his body see decay. God has raised this Jesus to life, and we are all witnesses of the fact." (Acts 2:30-32)

Peter then went on to apply Psalm 110 to the Lord Jesus (verses 34-35), and his final conclusion in verse 36 is:

"Therefore let all Israel be assured of this; God has made this Jesus, whom you crucified, both Lord and Christ."

David's Son was to be a priest for ever, in the order of Melchizedek (Psalm 110-4), and in the Epistle to the Hebrews we see this prophecy fulfilled in the Lord Jesus Christ:

"Christ also did not take upon himself the glory of becoming a high priest. But God said to him, 'You are my Son: today I have become your Father.' And he says in another place, 'You are a priest for ever, in the order of Melchizedek' … he (Jesus) became the source of eternal salvation for all who obey him and was designated by God to be high priest in the order of Melchizedek." (Hebrews 5:5-6, 9-10)

So the Lord Jesus Christ was the subject of these prophecies, though the nation of Israel refused to recognize this. The Lord's earthly ministry was rejected and He was put to death. When the message was repeated after His resurrection by the apostles, they still would not accept it and consequently Israel and the earthly purpose were set aside at the end of the book of Acts.

But this did not mean that God had abandoned His purpose for the nation of Israel, and through them for the nations of the earth. His promises to David and Abraham were unconditional and, since God cannot lie, He will fulfil His promises to His servants. When will He do this? We can learn something of this from Matthew 24 where the disciples asked the Lord:

> "… what will be the sign of your coming and of the end of the age?" (Matthew 24:3).

So the Lord's coming to set up His earthly Kingdom will be at the end of the age, and He will reign on the earth while Satan is imprisoned in the abyss for a thousand years (Revelation 20:2-6). But, as we have seen, this time of ruling on the earth will not be perfect. Judgments on Christ's enemies will take place. He will rule with a rod of iron, but, with Satan out of the way, there will be a measure of peace.

The earth, then, having witnessed the greatness of the Lord Jesus Christ when He came as the suffering Messiah of Israel, will one day see further aspects of His greatness when He comes in the role of the conquering King of Israel, dispensing justice and judgment on the earth for a thousand years.

But, at the end of the thousand years, what will happen? We are told in Revelation 20:7-10:

> "When the thousand years are over, Satan will be released from his prison and will go out to deceive the nations in the four corners of the earth – Gog and Magog – to gather them to battle...They marched across the breadth of the earth and surrounded the camp of God's people, the city he loves. But fire came down from heaven and devoured them. And the devil, who deceived them, was thrown into the lake of burning sulphur, where the beast and the false prophet had been thrown."

Satan will be out of action at last. No more will he spoil Christ's creation. Perfection and paradise can at last be restored.

> "Then I saw a new heaven and a new earth, for the first heaven and the first earth had passed away, and there was no longer any sea. I saw the Holy City, the new Jerusalem, coming down out of heaven

from God, prepared as a bride beautifully dressed for her husband. And I heard a loud voice from the throne saying, 'Now the dwelling of God is with men, and he will live with them. They will be his people, and God himself will be with them and be their God.'" (Revelation 21:1-3)

So here we have the Holy City, Jerusalem, the bride, the wife of the Lamb (the Lord Jesus), coming down to the new earth. God Himself declares:

> "I am the Alpha and the Omega, the Beginning and the End ... He who overcomes will inherit all this and I will be his God and he will be my son." (Revelation 21:6-7)

This is echoed by the Lord Jesus in the next chapter:

> "I am the Alpha and the Omega, the First and the Last, the Beginning and the End. Blessed are those who wash their robes,

that they may have the right to the tree of life and may go through the gates into the city." (Revelation 22:13-14)

Paradise will be restored, and the Lord Jesus Christ and the Lord God Almighty will reign and dwell with men. We see the Lord Jesus identified even more closely with God Himself, and the situation is summed up in Revelation 21:22-24:

> "I did not see a temple in the city, because the Lord God Almighty and the Lamb are its temple. The city does not need the sun or the moon to shine on it, for the glory of God gives it light, and the Lamb is its lamp. The nations will walk by its light, and the kings of the earth will bring their splendor into it."

What a beautiful picture! The whole world walking in the light of the heavenly city, which in turn basks in the light of God and the Lamb. The Lord Jesus Christ, by whom and for whom all things were created, will be Lord over perfection.

The Scriptures do not take us much further than this in relation to the earthly purpose. At the end of the millennium Satan will be cast into the lake of fire, and all Christ's enemies will be put down. Paul, in his first letter to the Corinthians, tells us something of the implications of the events described in Revelation 21 and 22:

> "Then the end will come, when he hands over the kingdom to God the Father after he has destroyed all dominion, authority and power. For he must reign until he has put all his enemies under his feet. The last enemy to be destroyed is death" (see Revelation 20:14)…"When he has done this, then the Son himself will be made subject to him who put everything under him, so that God may be all in all." (1 Corinthians 15:24-28).

It was God's will that everything should be put under Him, and one day this will be realized, though, as Hebrews 2:8 remarks:

"… at present we do not see everything subject to him."

When this does take place, "the end" will come when He hands over the Kingdom to God.

2. IN GOD'S HEAVENLY PURPOSE

The greatness of the risen Christ in relation to God's *earthly* purpose, then, has not yet been realized and, when we examine the prison epistles of the apostle Paul – especially Ephesians, Philippians and Colossians – and consider what he reveals there of the Lord's greatness in relation to God's *heavenly* purposes, it is not clear whether these have been fully realized at present or not. He speaks of the church as being seated:

> "… with him in heavenly realms in Christ Jesus." (Ephesians 2:6)

but this wonderful experience lies in the future for us, and at present we have the Spirit:

"… who is a deposit guaranteeing our inheritance until the redemption of those who are God's possession." (Ephesians 1:14)

We are potentially there, and Paul speaks in the same terms of the resurrection glories of Christ, so we shall consider them as a present reality.

As a result of the Lord Jesus Christ's willingness to humble Himself to the very depths, God's purposes were achieved. Therefore, Paul declares,

"God exalted him to the highest place and gave him the name that is above every name." (Philippians 2:9)

Paul is clear that the Lord was raised to these heights because of His obedience. He was able to look beyond His own suffering to the future glories that would follow when the Father's aims were achieved. The earlier New Testament epistles also make mention of the Lord's glorification in resurrection. For example Hebrews 12 states:

"Let us fix our eyes on Jesus, the author and perfector of our faith, who for the joy set before him endured the cross, scorning its shame, and sat down at the right hand of the throne of God." (verse 2)

In the same epistle, in the first chapter, a similar thought is expressed:

"After he had provided purification for sins, he sat down at the right hand of the Majesty in heaven. So he became as much superior to the angels as the name he has inherited is superior to theirs." (verses 3 and 4)

The Lord in resurrection is far superior to angelic beings, in contrast to His earthly life when He was

"… made a little lower than the angels." (Hebrews 2:9)

But Paul, in Ephesians 1, goes further, in speaking of the greatness of God's power he describes it as that:

"... which he exerted in Christ when he raised him from the dead and seated him at his right hand in the heavenly realms, far above all rule and authority, power and dominion, and every title that can be given, not only in the present age but also in the one to come." (verses 20-21)

There can be no created being higher than He, and God has raised Him to His rightful place as the creator and the goal of His creation. In Colossians 1:15, Paul describes the Lord in His work as creator as:

"... the firstborn over all creation."

In resurrection He is the firstborn in a different sense, as Paul declares in the same chapter (in verse 18):

"... he is the head of the body, the church; he is the beginning and the firstborn from among the dead."

He is the beginning. At the original creation, He was there as the creating power of God. Life under the old creation started with Him, and resurrection life starts with Him also. This leads Paul into describing the Lord as "the firstborn from among the dead".

Paul is not saying that Christ was the first person to be raised. The term "firstborn over all creation" did not mean that He was the first being to be created. It was a title of honor. In the same way "firstborn from the dead" is a title of honor. Just as He was the source of life under the old creation, so is He the source of life in resurrection. He has pride of place in the old creation and He has pride of place in the new. In particular, in God's heavenly purpose, He is head of the body, the Church. The very existence of the Church depends on Him, in two senses.

First, historically: If it had not been for the resurrection of the Lord Jesus Christ there would be no resurrection for believers either. This is a fundamental truth applicable to all Christians, in God's earthly or heavenly purposes. Paul, writing to the Corinthians, is careful to point out the importance of Christ's resurrection. In the fifteenth chapter of 1 Corinthians he declares:

> "… if Christ has not been raised, our preaching is useless and so is your faith." (verse 14)

To emphasize the point he repeats it in verse 17 and takes the issue further still:

> "… if Christ has not been raised, your faith is futile; you are still in your sins. Then those also who have fallen asleep in Christ are lost. If only for this life we have hope in Christ, we are to be pitied more than all men."

But that is not the end of the story. Paul continues triumphantly:

> "But Christ has indeed been raised from the dead, the firstfruits of those who have fallen asleep."

The picture of the Lord as the firstfruits is a very beautiful one. Under Old Testament law, the firstfruits of the harvest were always brought in and the sheaf waved before the Lord. In the same way, the Lord Jesus Christ was the firstfruits of the harvest of resurrection. He rose from the dead and ascended into the presence of His Father, and, in the same way, we will one day stand in the presence of God in our resurrection bodies, similar to His glorious body. So the Church has come into being only as a result of the resurrection work of Christ.

But there is a second sense in which the Church owes its existence to the Lord as Head. Its *continued* existence depends on the nourishment its members receive from the Lord in His capacity as Head. Writing to the Ephesians, Paul explains how we can grow up to be mature believers, not tossed back and forth like children by the deceits of men. In chapter 4 verse 15 he says:

> "Instead, speaking the truth in love, we will in all things grow up into him who is the Head, that is, Christ. Form him the whole

body, joined and held together by every supporting ligament, grows and builds itself up in love, as each part does its work."

By contrast, when Paul writes to warn the Colossian believers about the dangers of false teaching, and in particular the danger of legalism, he states that a person who delights in false humility and the worship of angels:

> "... has lost connection with the Head, from whom the whole body supported and held together by its ligaments and sinews, grows as God causes it to grow." (Colossians 2:19)

The Lord, in resurrection, was made Head of the Church, the body, and His work as Head is a continuing one, as He provides nourishment for the members of His body to grow until they:

> "... become mature, attaining to the whole measure of the fullness of Christ." (Ephesians 4:13)

Why did God choose to put the Lord Jesus in the high position? Paul goes on to tell us in Colossians 1:18. It was:

> "… so that in everything he might have the supremacy."

How total was this supremacy? Paul goes on:

> "For God was pleased to have all his fullness dwell in him".

The same thought recurs in the next chapter:

> "For in Christ all the fullness of the Deity lives in bodily form". (verse 9)

The full constitution of the Godhead is in Christ, and this peak has been reached in His resurrection. The Lord Jesus Christ then, in His resurrection glory, has been raised to the highest place, just as He was Lord of all in the original creation, so is He Lord of all in resurrection. The days of His humiliation are over. Paul ends the first chapter of Ephesians by telling us:

"And God placed all things under his feet and appointed him to be head over everything for the Church, which is his body, the fullness of him who fills everything in every way." (Ephesians 1:22-23)

These universals are beyond our comprehension, but it is clear that Paul is in no doubt that the risen Lord is far above all other beings in creation.

5.

CONCLUSION

CONCLUSION

God's purpose then, is to place the Lord Jesus Christ at the Head of His entire creation. Paul tells us in Ephesians 1:10 that God's purpose is:

> "… to be put into effect when the times will have reached their fulfilment – to bring all things in heaven and on earth together under one head, even Christ."

Writing to the Philippians, Paul goes further:

> "God exalted him to the highest place and gave him the name that is above every name, that at the name of Jesus every knee should bow, in heaven and on the earth and under the earth, and every tongue confess that Jesus Christ is Lord, to the glory of God the Father." (Philippians 2:9-11)

At the climax of God's earthly purpose we see the Lord dwelling on the new earth with men, who walk in His light, radiating from the heavenly city.

All Christ's enemies will have been destroyed and everything will be under His feet. He will be supreme over the earth.

In the heavens too, He is far above all. He is the firstborn from the dead (Colossians 1:18), and all the fullness of the Deity has its permanent dwelling in Him (Colossians 2:9). As in the earth, so in the heavens, all things are placed under His feet (Ephesians 1:22), and His supremacy is total.

* * * *

But how does this affect us living in the world? The wonder of it is that the life of a Christian is closely tied up with the Lord Jesus Christ. We are identified with Him in all that He has done. First, Romans chapter 6 teaches us that we died *with* Christ (Romans 6:8). But that is not all. Verse 11 of the same chapter tells us that we are to count ourselves dead to sin "but alive to God in Christ Jesus." We died to sin in Christ Jesus. Chapter 7 shows us that we also died to the law, *through* the body of Christ (Romans 7:4). We have deliverance from sin and the law, not because God decided to overlook our sin, but because we paid the penalty for our sin by dying *in Christ.* As Paul says in Romans 6:7 "anyone who has died has been freed from sin." We died with Him and are raised to "live a new life" with Him (Romans 6:4). Therefore Paul can conclude this section of Romans triumphantly in Chapter 8:

> "Therefore, there is now no condemnation for those who are *in Christ Jesus*, because *through Christ Jesus* the law of the Spirit of life set me free from the law of sin and death."

Our freedom from condemnation as sinners is only because we are *in Christ Jesus.*

Paul takes up this theme again in Ephesians, in the 2nd. Chapter, but here he goes further than in Romans:

> "And God raised us up with Christ and seated us with him in the heavenly realms *in Christ Jesus,* in order that in the coming ages he might show the incomparable

riches of his grace expressed in his kindness to us *in Christ Jesus* ... For we are God's workmanship, created *in Christ Jesus* to do good works, which God prepared in advance for us to do." (Ephesians 2:6-10)

Our preparedness for God's service as believers is only *in Christ Jesus.*

In the early chapters of Ephesians Paul brings out all that God has done for us in and through the Lord Jesus Christ. We are blessed in the heavenly realms with every spiritual blessing *in Christ* (1:3). We are chosen *in Him* before the creation of the world (1:4). We are predestinated to be adopted as His sons *through Christ Jesus* (!:5). *In Him* we have redemption (1:7). *In Him* we are chosen to be to the praise of His glory (1:11-12). We are made alive *with Christ* (2:5), raised and seated *with Christ* (2:6). In fact all that we are, or can ever hope to be is in Christ, so that Paul can sum up the position of Christian believers in Colossians 3 by saying:

"Since, then, you have been raised with Christ, set your hearts on things above, where Christ is seated at the right hand of God. …For you died, and youR life is now hidden with Christ in God. When Christ, who is your life, appears, then you also will appear with him in glory." (Colossians 3:1-4)

So closely are we linked with the Lord Jesus that Paul describes Him as "your life". He is the Head, not only over all creation but particularly over everything for the Church which is His body, and, as members of His body, we draw our sustenance *from Him* rather than from the celebration of rituals or other "religious" acts which:

"… are a shadow of the things that were to come; the reality, however, is found in Christ." (Colossians 2:17)

If we do this we will grow. Paul teaches us in Ephesians 4 that:

"From him the whole body, joined and held together by every supporting ligament, grows and builds itself up in love, as each part does its work." (verse 16)

In dealing with the Lord's resurrection glories we saw that Paul teaches that: "all the fullness of Deity lives in bodily form" in Christ; (Colossians 2:9).

But there is a parallel here for the members of His body. In the next verse Paul adds "and you have been given fullness in Christ". In Ephesians 1:23 Paul describes the Church as "the fullness of him who fills everything in every way." Just as the fullness of God dwells bodily in Christ, so the fullness of Christ dwells "bodily" in the Church. What does this mean for us in practical terms?

When God looks at us He sees us in Christ and our standing in Christ is secure. We are complete *in Him*. But there is also a sense in which we are expected to grow to maturity, not to remain as spiritual babies. In Ephesians 4 Paul explains that

Christ appointed apostles, prophets, evangelists, pastors and teachers. For what purpose?

> "To prepare God's people for works of service, so that the body of Christ may be built up until we all reach unity in the faith and in the knowledge of the Son of God and become mature, attaining to the whole measure of the fullness of Christ." (Ephesians 4:12-13)

When we reach that stage we shall no longer be infants, blown here and there by every wind of teaching, as Paul goes on to say, Instead we will grow up into our Head, the Lord Jesus Christ (verse 15).

So the Lord Jesus Christ stands supreme as the "chief cornerstone" of God's purposes concerning the heavens and the earth, and we are linked with Him in His death, burial, resurrection, ascension and glorification, and if we maintain and develop our links with Him, He will dwell in our hearts through faith, to the end that we may ...

"… be made complete
in accordance with
God's own standard of completeness."
(Ephesians 3:19 - Weymouth).

ALSO ON CHRIST

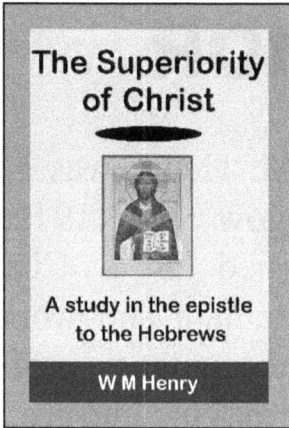

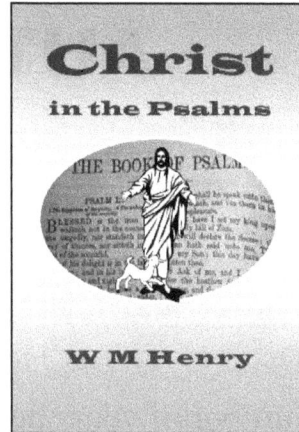

The Superiority of Christ
A study in the epistle to the Hebrews
By W M Henry

Christ in the Psalms
By W M Henry

These, and all the publications mentioned in this book, can be ordered from **www.obt.org.uk** or

The Open Bible Trust, Fordland Mount, Upper Basildon, Reading, RG8 8LU, UK.

They are also available as eBooks from Amazon and Apple and as KDP paperbacks from Amazon

ABOUT THE AUTHOR

W. M. Henry was born in Glasgow in 1949. He qualified as a Chartered Accountant and worked in the accountancy profession for a number of years before moving into academia. He is now retired and lives in Giffnock with his wife and two daughters. He is an international speaker and has spoken in Canada, Australia and the Netherlands. He has recently had published a major book, *The Trinity in John*: see later for details.

Other publications by W M Henry include:

The Signs in John's Gospel
Covenants: Old and New
No Condemnation – Romans 5:12-8:39
Living in the Truth
That you may know – 1 John
The Speeches in Acts
By Faith Abraham
The Making of a Man of God
Imitating Christ

W M henry has also written a number of books with Michael Penny including:

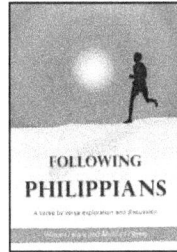

Who is Jesus?
A study based on Matthew 16:13-16

The Will of God: Past and Present.
In the Bible and in the 21st Century

Sit! Walk! Stand!
The Christian life in Ephesians

Following Philippians
A verse by verse exploration and discussion

Further details of these can be seen on
www.obt.org.uk
And they can be ordered from that website

W M Henry is a frequent contributor to *Search* magazine

ALSO BY
W M HENRY

The Trinity in John
A study in relationships

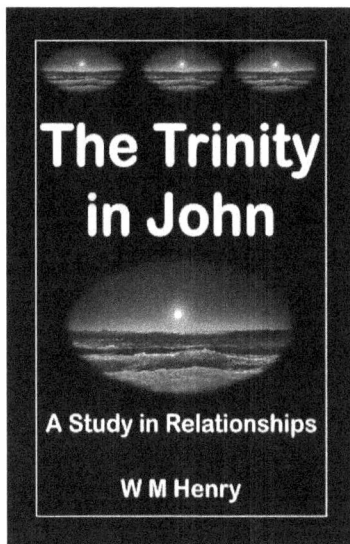

This book is a study of the relationships between the members of the Trinity and between the Trinity and Christian believers, focusing mainly on the Gospel of John.

It opens with a discussion of the titles given to the Lord Jesus in John's Gospel and what they tell us about His relationship with His Father.

Section two explores the relationship between the Father and the Son and their joint work of redemption.

The book then widens the focus to examine the relationship between the Father, the Son and the believer before discussing the Holy Spirit and His relationship with other members of the Trinity, and with the believer.

Each chapter closes with brief meditative "Reflections" on the implications of the issues raised in the chapter. These are followed by suggestions for further study, which can be the basis for private devotions or group discussions.

****

About this book

The Greatness of Christ

In this publication W M Henry deals with a subject which is dear to the heart of every Christians – the *greatness* of his Saviour. He considers:

- Christ's greatness before Bethlehem;
- His greatness while on earth; and
- His greatness in resurrection: with respect to God's earthly purpose and His heavenly purpose.

Publications of The Open Bible Trust must be in accordance with its evangelical, fundamental and dispensational basis. However, beyond this minimum, writers are free to express whatever beliefs they may have as their own understanding, provided that the aim in so doing is to further the object of The Open Bible Trust. A copy of the doctrinal basis is available at

www.obt.org.uk/doctrinal-basis

or from:

THE OPEN BIBLE TRUST
Fordland Mount, Upper Basildon,
Reading, RG8 8LU, UK

www.ingramcontent.com/pod-product-compliance
Lightning Source LLC
Chambersburg PA
CBHW070545030426
42337CB00016B/2364